HEY!

IT'S O.K.
TO GROW OLD

A LOVING LOOK AT LIFE IN A MODERN
RETIREMENT COMMUNITY

written by
SHERRY CONOHAN

Dedication

This book is dedicated to the late Tom Duffy,
a professor at the University of Missouri
School of Journalism and the toughest editor
I ever had, who taught me the basics
of how to be a good journalist.

Foreword

The names of the people and places in this book, including that of the retirement community depicted, are fictitious with the exception of an occasional reference to a big city. But the experiences are real. I made a very happy move to a modern retirement community and was inspired to write about it in this book to provide the reader some insight into what life can be like in such a facility and share the joy of the carefree days people can have as they move into their senior years.

--Sherry Conohan

Table of Contents

*"Those who live in Palm Acres
came to enjoy the good life"*

1
Chapter One
Welcome

Outside, the palm fronds rustled in a gentle breeze and provided a smidgen of shade for the walking paths below. Inside, in the well-appointed dining room, diners were helping themselves to the freshly made shrimp salad, tuna salad, potato salad and other tasty offerings in the popular salad bar while others chose to order off the menu.

It was lunch time in the Palm Acres retirement community and many of those eating at that hour had come from a morning activity or were going to one afterwards.

Scanning the room, one could not help but notice that they were not the only one who has some difficulty standing up after sitting for a while.

A few of the residents would place their hands on the table for support as they pulled themselves up from their chair. They then would stand for a few moments in place, steadying themselves, before slowly moving away from the table.

It was one reminder – a very small one – that this is a place where the population is older, as it is where people have come to retire. For the most part they are a very healthy lot. They run, they swim, they play tennis, they play golf, they ride bikes – and trikes.

Even so, there is a smattering of walkers and canes being used. But those relying on them for a little help will tell you they get around just fine, thank you, and prove it.

Those who live in Palm Acres came to enjoy the good life. Residents one meets when visiting it while looking for a retirement community will happily say they are being spoiled – and they love being spoiled. All the maintenance – outside and inside – of the buildings where they live, whether apartments, villas or "cottages" as the stand-alone homes are called, is taken care of by management as part of the monthly fee. Also included in that fee is all utilities except telephone and, in the houses, electricity. The fee includes weekly housekeeping, laundering of sheets and towels, one meal a day for each day of the month (i.e. 30 meals in a 30-day month) and transportation by car to anywhere you want to go in town or nearby. Valets are available during the dinner hour to park your car if you have driven to the clubhouse and retrieve it for you after dinner.

You want a picture hung, closet shelves adjusted, a clogged sink or toilet cleared, a light bulb changed? You pick up the phone and call maintenance and someone to do the job is soon at the door.

And, of course, all landscaping of the gorgeous grounds is included.

All this and tipping is forbidden. An employee would be fired for accepting a tip.

The staff, resident hosts will tell you, are wonderful and will do anything for you.

"What's there not to like about Palm Acres?" is a question often asked rhetorically by residents showing guests around.

The weather is another plus. A good portion of members – as residents are called – have left harsher northern climes to come to Palm Acres. It's far enough south, however to offer some colorful creatures with which to share the neighborhood.

One of them is announced on a sign just inside the gate to the larger community.

Attached to the speed limit sign, just below the "25" mile an hour notice, is another sign warning, "Don't feed alligators."

There's a certain cachet to that.

Not every retirement community serves up alligators, but many modern retirement communities offer such services and amenities as Palm Acres. These communities are not the "home" of your grandparents' era, but could pass for vacation retreats.

The adult children of some residents have been known to be appalled upon hearing mom and dad are moving into a retirement place, thinking the worst, then when they visit and see the beautiful surroundings and the lovely housing, they go "Ahhhh, now we understand."

It doesn't hurt that it has a swimming pool, a small golf course and a lot of activities for the parents to enjoy.

No, there's nothing to fear from the modern retirement communities. There's only joy that the "home" of old is now accompanied by a more upscale type of residence.

*"The dogs instinctively know
we're going to the beach
and go on high alert"*

2
Chapter Two
Who's Got Fleas?

One of the most delightful activities at Palm Acres retirement community is the Monday morning beach walk.

The inveterate beach walkers among us – usually a dozen strong, give or take one or two each week – don our sneakers and clamber aboard one of our buses at 9:30 a.m. for the short drive to the beach we favor.

About half of our number bring their dogs with them, which makes this outing particularly enjoyable – and one of my favorite activities since moving in.

The dogs instinctively know we're going to the beach and go on high alert, twitching in anticipation of the opportunity to run freely and dive into the gentle waves.

The itchiest is Buddy, a yellow lab mix with some hound in him who was adopted out of a shelter at six months and was in full blown puppyhood when we first met. His owner, who had lost her beloved mastiff only a few months earlier, was just beginning her struggle to teach him some manners. He is the sweetest dog, but was rambunctious and full of the dickens when he began going to the beach soon after the first of the year. He flunked obedience training – twice.

Buddy loves racing up and down the beach and frolicking in the water. Never mind that it was January.

Other four-footed friends who accompany us on the beach

include Marty, Cody, Sassy, Daisy and Teddy Bear, a teacup poodle and the tiniest among them at 3 ½ pounds, who delicately tiptoes across the sand in lady-like fashion by the side of her owner. She chooses, with good reason, not to go into the ocean.

The human beachgoers go off in different directions – some one way, some the other, the dog owners following their pet's lead. They move at a healthy clip or a more leisurely pace, whichever they find more comfortable.

Everyone winds up back at our beachhead where we've set up some folding beach chairs for anyone who would like to just sit and read, or soak up the sun or take in the view, in time for an 11 a.m. departure for our return home.

A few weeks later after that first outing for me, a bigger bus than our usual one pulled up in front of the clubhouse to pick up the beach walkers. When our driver was asked why the larger bus he explained that when our regular bus was used to transport residents to another activity, one of those who had been aboard later complained there were fleas on it. As a result, our regular bus was taken out of service to be fumigated.

The dog owners among our beach walkers were indignant. They said none of their dogs had fleas!

3

Chapter Three
Edith

I met Edith over dinner early-on after my arrival at Palm Acres in December. She had been pointed out to me from afar earlier with some reverence and I was told she was 103 years old.

Edith was sharp as a tack as we talked over dinner – there were no cobwebs on that brain – and her only concession to the encroaching years was the use of a walker to get around and she walked spryly with it.

During our conversation Edith made mention that she played bridge – not just party bridge, but duplicate bridge. I took BIG note of that. All I could think of was all the years of practice she had at the game over her 103 years and feared the day I would play against her.

I didn't at the time think about playing WITH her. But I should have.

One Wednesday afternoon when we were playing bridge with the party group and she was my partner for a time (we changed partners after every six hands), I stopped my bidding at the two level. Edith played the hand and went on to make a grand slam – which, thanks to me, we had not bid.

She was NOT pleased.

*"Edith played the hand and went
on to make a grand slam"*

4

Chapter Four
Save the Bird

In January, after the Christmas rush had passed, I began to attend the meetings of the regime board and the member committees of Palm Acres.

At a meeting of the Members' Council – a group consisting of a representative of each of the other committees – it was reported that thought was being given to converting the fountain with a bird spouting water on the patio outside the bar and dining room into a flower bed. The reason: The fountain had a crack in the bottom of it.

I was appalled and said so at the meeting. I loved that fountain. It was beautiful!

When I told my new friends about the plan, they too were appalled.

I told Julia about the proposal one day when we were sitting on the patio and she was sputtering she was so angry. "I'll sit on it," she said of the bird, "so they can't take it away."

And I didn't think, Julia, who was 89 and used a walker, was entirely joking.

Thankfully, when the committee met in February, it was reported the plan to turn the fountain into a flower bed had been scrapped. The crack in the bottom would be fixed.

Cooler heads had prevailed.

"I'll sit on it," she said of the bird,
"so they can't take it away"

5

Chapter Five
A Close Call

When you live in an old folks home, albeit a very nice one like Palm Acres, you can expect some or your neighbors and friends are going to get sick or die.

My first such scare occurred with Julia, but fortunately it was a brief episode.

Julia and I had plans to have dinner together on a Monday night early in February. But during that day she called to say she didn't feel well and had to cancel. We then made plans to have dinner together a few days later on Thursday.

I called her on Wednesday to see how she felt and to remind her of our dinner date. She said she felt somewhat worse, but expected to be okay to go to dinner the next day.

On Thursday, I was out all afternoon but shortly after I got home around 5 p.m. I received a phone call from our concierge who said Julia had called her and asked her to call me to tell me she wouldn't be meeting me for dinner because she was in the hospital. She had gone to the doctor that afternoon and he sent her straight from his office to the hospital.

I was concerned because not only is Julia elderly and walks with the aid of a walker, but she has a pacemaker and can hardly see. I suddenly saw her as mortal.

Blessedly, Julia was okay. After a cautionary overnight stay in the hospital, she came home following dinner the next day. Her daughter and son-in-law, who live nearby, had been at her bedside from soon after she arrived at the hospital and brought her home.

6
Chapter Six
Death Comes Calling

Death, however, touched someone close to me only a couple of months after I arrived at Palm Acres.

The husband of a friend died on Valentine's Day after waging a gallant fight against cancer.

I really didn't know him since he had been pretty sick since I moved in, but I had become friendly with his wife, a lovely woman.

Chuck had been moved into our health center for hospice care two weeks earlier and his wife and their children, who had been summoned from points north, had been keeping a vigil by his bedside.

The funeral – a memorial service - was held a couple of days later and a huge crowd turned out, a testament to how respected and loved Chuck was.

He and his wife had lived in a nearby neighborhood before moving to Palm Acres and he had been in involved in many community committees and local charities. People at the memorial service came from all those walks of his life, as well as Palm Acres.

Chuck's daughter delivered a beautiful and moving tribute to her father and the clergyman conducted a lovely service, commending Chuck's devotion to family and his contributions to the community.

The family held a reception back at Palm Acres afterwards and as often happens at wakes, some good stories were swapped among the guests.

One came from a man who had lived in a house on a nearby golf course. He said golf balls were constantly being hit through windows of the house. One time a golf ball came sailing through a window of the bathroom while his wife was in the tub. Unbelievably, the guy who hit it came to the front door and asked if he could have his ball back.

The fellow had his own idea about who was hitting the balls through his widows. He said they were being hit by men who were being macho, having to show off how far they could hit a ball. They hit the ball far, but had no control.

The women, he said, weren't trying for distance. They didn't hit their balls as far, but hit them straight.

Eventually, this fellow said, he replaced all the windows in his house with unbreakable glass like that used in banks, only not quite as thick as that in the banks.

The downside of this move, he went on, was the glass would turn yellow under the heat of the sun.

This man and his wife, finally deciding they had had enough, have since moved to a house on a peaceful waterway close by where they now sit outside and watch the tug boats and pleasure boats go by.

7

Chapter Seven
Fitness and Sports

From the well-equipped fitness room to the swimming pool to the three-hole golf course to the wide-range of exercise classes, there is plenty of opportunity for residents of Palm Acres to stay fit or to get fit.

And it's all included in the monthly fee. There is no additional "amenities" charge.

The always busy fitness room has more than a dozen apparatus and the retirement community's energetic and helpful fitness coordinator will work up a regimen specific to the individual and what he or she wants to accomplish.

There are no sign-ups, but when people are waiting to get on a machine, those using them are asked to give theirs up after 20 minutes and wait until another opens up.

In addition to workouts on the apparatus, the fitness coordinator conducts a number of classes such as "sit and be fit" (four days a week), a balance class (three days a week), a low impact aerobics class, a more challenging aerobics class and an "abs... abs...abs" abdominal exercise class (two days a week).

She also conducts a water aerobics class five days a week in the year-round heated pool which has a top that is closed in winter and rolls open in summer, and leads the Monday morning beach walk – among many other activities.

Outside instructors teach yoga, Qigong, chair Zumba and line dancing classes.

The duffers among residents can practice their putts on one of the holes of the golf course or make it a nine-hole game by going around the three-hole course three times. On one Saturday of the month, teams of residents compete against one another.

There also is an active croquet crowd (serious business), bocce and Wii bowling.

All in all, there's plenty to keep the senior crowd a healthy and fit lot.

8

Chapter Eight
The Golf Tournament

What a beautiful day and what a beautiful golf course! They do the month of April proud.

Golf courses abound in the area around my retirement community but this was considered the premier course and the tournament was a major one in the national men's tour. Both were a first for me and it would be a grand outing.

One of the founders of Palm Acres, who is still active in the management, has for several years taken a skybox at one of the holes to treat prospective buyers of homes in the complex and many of the members who like golf to a front row seat to see the tourney action.

He entertains his guests with a lovely catered lunch and open bar while they sit in tiered rows of chairs and watch the players try to beat the Par 4 assigned to that hole. Only one player did during the afternoon I was there – one of the two leaders who were the last pair to play the hole for the day.

This was the first golf tournament I had ever attended. While I have watched golf on television, I quickly learned there was a lot going on that never gets caught by the cameras.

It ranges from the volunteers who hold up elongated "Quiet" signs, much like the state signs you see at a national political conventions, just before each player is about to hit the ball, to the frequent tossing of golf balls between players and their caddies. The throws go in both directions. Some of the tosses were overhand. Some were underhand. Either way, nobody missed. There was no dropped ball.

To get to the green where we sat, the players had to hit over a sand trap that lies just in front of the green. A few balls didn't make it to the green, but most of those players were very adept at hitting out of the sand to a good lie on the green in one shot.

The green was deceptive in its appearance. It looked smooth with just a small slant to it, but it harbored some nasty curves that were not readily apparent and many of the players saw their balls break just shy of the hole on one side or the other.

There was a lighted billboard just to our right that alerted us to approaching players and flashed the standings frequently. It also gave steady reminders to visitors to turn off their cell phones. We had no offender in that category. But on occasion someone in our box would continue talking after the "Quiet" sign went up, which drew immediate "shushes" from those around them.

On hand to help make the experience a pleasant and memorable one were the four members of the Palm Acres marketing department and two department managers. They kept the food and drink flowing and assisted those looking for seats and going up and down the stairs.

When play on the links was concluded, the crowd gave a hearty "thank you" to our community's founder who had been our host before leaving the skybox and boarding he buses that brought us for the ride home. It had been a day to remember.

9

Chapter Nine
Reverie – Spring

As I sit at a high top table on the deck of my favorite watering hole sipping a glass of wine, I look over the band of marsh grass at the water's edge to the waterway beyond and marvel at how beautiful this new place I call home is.

The deck is shaded by huge live oak trees, their branches dripping with Spanish moss, and a light breeze stirs the air, making my perch comfortable even with the temperature hovering at 100 degrees.

Lovely palm trees rise from the soil on either of the deck, intermixed with frond-laden tropical plants, making the whole scene look like a slice of Paradise.

Stretching out into the water to the left and the right are two long boardwalks leading to two docks where a handful of small to medium-sized boats are tied up.

Herons, white and blue, with their elegant long necks, sit on top of most of the pilings to which the floating docks are attached, hoping for scraps from the fishermen cleaning their catch.

What is a blue heron, you may ask? I am told it is any heron that is not white. It may be brown, or black – or even blue.

A server from an adjacent bar and eatery to my right passes by on the path in front of my deck holding a tray up by one hand with half a dozen drinks for the boating folks now sitting at a large round wrought iron table on the dock to my left.

Further to the left, a shrimp boat lies tied up to the dock at yet another bar and restaurant which has a fish market on site. Its sky blue hull barely moves in the water, revealing only a sliver of the terra cotta red belly below.

On the boardwalk to the dock on the right, a forklift that lowers boats into the water and raises them from it trundles out to the end to retrieve a boat with Bimini top that's headed for dry dock – at least temporarily.

It is a languid day with no boat traffic in the channel, save for a lone passing shrimper.

This is the South on a hot, humid day when the locals are hunkering down, mostly in air conditioning.

As I gaze over the broad body of water, I am reminded how uplifting it is every time I drive over the bridge from the mainland, two bridges really, to the island that now is home. Look to the left, look to the right, and you see the Lowcountry express itself. Its natural beauty is breathtaking.

I am now like my neighbors in my retirement community who say they look forward to driving over that bridge when returning from a vacation, with its magnificent views over the marsh and water, because it reminds them how fortunate they are to live on this little corner of the Earth.

10

Chapter Ten
A Lifestyle Choice

One can be as busy or un-busy as one wants at Palm Acres. Besides all the exercises and sports that are available to residents, there is a slew of other activities to choose from. The retirement community's tireless and extremely resourceful activities director offers up an amazing array of things to do every month.

Staples on the calendar include "restaurant of the month," which could be either dinner or lunch, when everyone who wants to go piles on a bus and heads out for a good time, and the movie of the month, providing there's a good flick playing nearby.

There also are outings to the local symphony orchestra, which is a first class outfit, and to productions of local community theaters and to shows of the occasional touring companies from New York City, also to see operas performed by the New York Metropolitan Opera which are broadcast live to a local movie theater.

Art movies, and recent releases of contemporary movies we missed at the theaters are shown in the community's large meeting hall, accompanied by popcorn, and then are aired over Palm Acres' in-house television station to everyone's home.

Wine and cheese mixers are regular fare and a longtime nightclub performer, now semi-retired, appears often to entertain everyone with a little cabaret piano and song.

There are member-staff tennis tournaments and member-staff golf tournaments, which are held at the neighborhood rec center tennis courts and a local country club's golf course. There also is a member art and craft show where everyone learns how immensely talented many of our neighbors on campus are.

Palm Acres also brings in guest lecturers on various subjects and invites in trunk shows to display their clothing so members can shop without having to leave home.

No one wants to miss the big Kentucky Derby party, with prizes for the most outstanding hats. Or if tennis is one's game, there's the Breakfast at Wimbledon party for the men's final with traditional English treats such as strawberries and cream.

No holiday goes uncelebrated. There are grand cookouts with hamburgers and hotdogs grilled outdoors and all the picnic dishes to go with them for Memorial Day, 4th of July and Labor Day. There are lavish holiday meals with all the trimmings for Thanksgiving, Christmas, New Year's Eve and New Year's Day. Hanukkah also is observed and there are special meals for St. Patrick's Day and Valentine's Day.

Residents of Palm Acres are not confined by their immediate surroundings. They travel farther afield to catch shows in Charlotte, N.C., and Jacksonville, Fla. They go to Atlanta, Ga., in the spring to see a Braves baseball game – different opponents in different years – and take in some of the city's finer establishments. In January or February, there's the annual Caribbean cruise – different islands in different years.

These are all Palm Acres' trips. But a host of other trips, all escorted, are offered through the retirement community's association with a travel agency that will pick up members at their residence to take them to the airport and bring them home afterward.

If all of this information has your head swimming, don't worry. Some people may choose a quieter lifestyle, relaxing at home, sunning themselves by the pool, working one of the jigsaw puzzles always in the works in the lobbies of the apartment and villa buildings, or just reading a good book – maybe one from the Palm Acres library.

There's a book discussion group for those interested in doing that.

It's your choice. But no one can complain that there's nothing to do.

*"a longtime nightclub performer,
now semi-retired, appears often
to entertain everyone with a little
cabaret piano and song"*

11

Chapter Eleven
Art Imitates Life

Every once in a while a movie comes along that really touches the audience. So it was with "The Best Exotic Marigold Hotel" and the Palm Acres residents who saw it.

This was no ordinary movie, at least not for these seniors who have retired.

It is about a bunch of Brits who left England for retirement in India in what they discover when they get there was a dilapidated hotel – The Best Exotic Marigold Hotel.

Our number filled the 26 passenger big bus run by Palm Acres for trips and major events. As retirees, everyone was interested in finding out what it was about this movie that made everyone who had seen it rave so about it.

It turned out to be both very funny and soberingly serious. Two big attractions for our group coming into the movie were the British female stars – Judi Dench and Maggie Smith, both of whom did not disappoint. But the entire ensemble, consisting of several other well-known actors and actresses, was outstanding.

Another star of the show was the background scenery – the streets of India's cities teeming with gazillions of people and saturated with color. I have never had any desire to go to India and after seeing this movie, wild horses couldn't drag me there. It was appalling.

But the movie, after a somewhat slow start, got into its groove and what a groove it was.

There were people falling in love, falling out of love and finding a way to surmount a mother's objection to their love. There also was unrequited love.

The movie also touched on such senior issues as a newly minted widow struggling to find her way without a husband who had always done everything for them, and a lonely man searching for female companionship while worrying about his virility.

And death. One of their number who had grown up in India and loved it returned to the country with the desire to die there when the grim reaper came calling.

It was a stunning show. Everyone raved about it as we left the theater. A few vowed to see it a second time.

The consensus was the movie deserved an Oscar from the Academy Awards – actually several of them – for Best Picture, Best Director, Best Screenplay, maybe some actors, even though it was an ensemble cast, and who knows what else.

But, we asked, is it eligible for the regular Oscars or must it be put in the foreign film category? That is the question. It is billed as a British comedy-drama.

Alas, when the Academy Award nominations were announced there was none for "The Best Exotic Marigold Hotel."

12

Chapter Twelve
Games People Play

Bridge, without a doubt, is the most popular card game on the Palm Acres campus. Bridge games are going on every morning, afternoon and evening.

The planned activities at Palm Acres include duplicate bridge competitive play on Tuesday afternoons and party bridge on Wednesday afternoons. But private bridge games can be found underway at all times of the day and evening, some in the public rooms of the clubhouse that have been booked for them, and other times in residents' homes and apartments.

You don't know how to play bridge but would like to learn, no problem. Lessons teaching basic bridge are available as an activity. So are lessons for those who already play bridge but want to improve their skill at bidding.

Other card games played regularly in the retirement community are canasta, gin rummy and poker – the latter a mostly guy thing.

Another popular game is mah jongg, played on different days in different places.

A game that fills the large meeting hall in the clubhouse once a month is Bingo. All participants are allowed to play two cards and the retirement community's fitness director chooses the games and calls the numbers.

Two winners are allowed per game except for the final game which calls for covering an entire card. Only one winner is allowed unless two or more bingos are called out at the same time.

Games range from regular bingo to regular bingo with all four corners, to the six-pack, or the kite, to other innovations that keep the players happy.

Residents organize in teams for trivia night, with teams competing against one another. Points are awarded for each answer a team gets right and the team with the most points at the evening's end wins bragging rights as having the best informed folks on campus – until the next trivia night and then its show time again.

13

Chapter Thirteen

Music, Music, Music

The underlying glue that unites all that everyone does at Palm Acres is the music.

Music becomes part of the lives of the residents with all the programs and performances that are lined up by the activities director. It is not uncommon to have as many as four musical treats, in-house, in one week. With two big concert pianos, one the gift of a resident, there is no end to the musical fare that can be produced.

There is a couple who comes every year and plays duets on the piano. There is another couple – a woman who sings and a man who accompanies her on the piano – who draw from years of playing with the big bands and in Las Vegas who entertain. There is the previously mentioned former night club performer who appears regularly.

There also is the opportunity to hear some of the contestants in an international youth piano competition and a youth concerto competition strut their stuff under our roof. They are amazingly talented young people that can blow a listener away.

A Big Band from the neighborhood just outside the retirement community comes over from time to time to play all the old favorites such as Satin Doll and My Funny Valentine. The soaring trumpet solo from My Funny Valentine is a show stopper.

We go out to musical events as well, such as "Razzle Dazzle" and "Hearts Afire" which are home grown variety shows featuring men barber shoppers and a women's singing group, along with other performers. It's always fun.

There also are trips to professional touring musical shows from New York such as "Anything Goes," "The Rat Pack" and "9 to 5." The Choral Society presents several shows throughout the year including one with a patriotic theme for Memorial Day.

One of the developers of Palm Acres has sponsored a wonderful concert for a couple of years running for residents of Palm Acres featuring an outstanding, enormously talented – and very entertaining – professional pianist. It is held in the local arts center, which always is packed with residents of the retirement community.

The pianist brings an equally talented singer with him.

When our activities director went to a conference of other people working in the same field held in the Southwest, she was appalled to find a new retirement home there that she visited had no piano. She kept looking for a piano, but there was none. She couldn't believe it. Music is so much a part of our life.

14

Chapter Fourteen

The Two Sides of Technology

Here we are cruising along happily in life when technology comes along to disrupt – in the opinion of some - our way of doing things.

One has to keep in mind that the population of Palm Acres did not grow up in the computer age. Many members have adapted to it, but others have not.

The technology issue arose when a member of the retirement community who worked closely with computers in his business life decided the way business is run at Palm Acres should be updated a bit.

His first venture really was not controversial. He devised a computerized format for our trivia games. Up until then, the questions were read aloud by the activities director and the competing teams wrote their answer from a choice of possibilities on a piece of paper. The teams then exchanged their answer sheets and marked the scores.

With the computerized version, a large movie screen and remote controls are used. The questions are posted on the screen and each team presses the button on their remote control with the appropriate number to file their answer. When all answers have been filed to a question, the overseer presses a button to show the winning answer.

The computer then goes to work and notes which team or teams have the right answer and keeps count of the points that team gets for that question. The questions are weighted according to their difficulty, which goes up as the game goes along. Everyone seems to like the new improved version.

Our computer wiz has taken over the creation of the questions and the multiple choice of answers to them, plugging them into the computer, and has done an excellent job of presenting a fine array of subjects in the game to challenge our brains.

His other project has not had as harmonious a reception. He has created an in-house computer system by which members are supposed to do most everything on the computer – make reservations for dinner, sign up for trips, sign up for outings to the theater and elsewhere, sign up for golf carts, etc.

Dinner reservations are now made by phone or in person with the dining room and members put their names on sign-up sheets at the activities desk for the others.

Management has embraced this move to computerize nearly everything.

Reaction among residents is mixed, divided about half and half between those who support it and those who are opposed.

Home computers were set to connect with this system and computers were set up in the lobbies of the apartment and villa buildings for the use of people without a computer.

As it turned out, glitches were found when the new computerized system was rolled out and it has been put on hold while an effort is made to correct the problems.

15

Chapter Fifteen
Dinner Anyone?

Dinner at Palm Acres is a social occasion as well as a dining experience.

It takes place in both a lovely formal dining room and a more informal bistro. There is a dress code for each which is adjusted for winter and summer months.

Between the two lies a busy cocktail lounge where many members relax and visit with one another before dinner over a glass of wine, a martini, a Scotch, a Jack Daniels – or a Sunset, a favorite non-alcoholic drink - before going in to their tables.

Palm Acres, blessedly, has open seating for dinner. Some senior facilities have assigned seating where one is required to spend this social time with the same people day in and day out for a certain period, after which they switch dining partners.

With open seating comes the responsibility to make a reservation for dinner. One may be invited to join others at their table, but it also sometimes falls upon you to organize your own table. This requires a modicum of an outgoing personality, which does not come easily to everyone. But the residents are a friendly lot and will help.

When a new member moves in, invitations flow to that person from other residents, inviting the new person to join them at their tables. Members of the Welcoming Committee particularly reach out to them. In time, as the new member settles in and meets his or her new neighbors, they become able to form their own dinner groups.

The alternative is dining alone, which some people find even more daunting, or ordering dinner sent over to your apartment or house. It should be said that people order dinner in for a lot of reasons – they are ill, their don't feel like going out that day, or they have work to do at home and don't want to take the time to go to the dining room.

Some people choose to go to dinner late so they can see the evening news on television. The downside of that is there are fewer people to eat with at that hour.

An unscientific observation indicates that couples tend to eat with other couples, single women tend to eat with other single women, and, ditto, single men tend to eat with other single men. Having said that, however, they also often mix it up.

What they all share is a good meal. The food served at Palm Acres is excellent.

16

Chapter Sixteen
Reverie – Fall

It is fall now and this is an absolutely gorgeous day – a clear blue sky without a cloud in it, low to no humidity and the temperature is mild in the upper 60s.

Gone is the clammy heat of summer when sometimes the air was so hot and close that one found it hard to breathe

I am back at my favorite watering hole and happier than ever. The waterway in front of me is a mill pond and the huge, magnificent live oaks still drip with Spanish moss.

I have traveled afar since arriving here – to Chicago, to Detroit to pick up a cruise through the Great Lakes and the St. Lawrence Seaway up to Quebec City, and to a couple of Southern cities to explore – and now have experienced the joy my friends have described of going over that bridge to my island and seeing the beautiful marsh stretching out in either direction.

I don't see any herons sitting on the pilings at this hour but it is late in the day and they may be back in their nests. Only one small boat has pulled into the dock, but then it would be late for the pleasure boaters too.

I spent the afternoon in a sports bar where I could see my beloved Giants play since their games aren't regularly broadcast on local television. I watched as the marvelous Eli Manning pulled one of his trademark late in the fourth quarter heart-stopping histrionics to post a win over the scrappy Washington Redskins, one of our division rivals.

In my euphoria over this stunning victory, and in light of the beautiful afternoon, I decided to cap off the day with a stop enroute home at my favorite watering hole.

The deck is filling with people arriving for cocktails and dinner and one of the servers has lighted the little butane torches that line the railing separating us from the water. Darkness is not yet falling, but it will soon. The days grow shorter and shorter.

Soon the holidays will be upon us with Thanksgiving, Christmas and New Year's – bang, bang, bang – and my one year anniversary of living in Paradise will roll around.

I thank the good Lord every day for leading me here.

17

Chapter Seventeen
An Illness Strikes Back

Julia did well initially when she returned home from the hospital after the scare she had, but problems soon developed.

I wasn't the only one scared by Julia's hospital episode. Her family was too. The all flew in to see her the following week after she was back home. This included her two other daughters besides the one who lives locally. When they got here they found their mother reasonably healthy and in good spirits – her old self.

Alas that did not last. The problems that developed kept her shuffling between the hospital and the nursing home on the grounds of Palm Acres. Eventually, a panel of health professionals told Julia they felt she could no longer live independently.

By this time, she was on oxygen full-time and in a weakened condition. But she still had her old spirit.

By the time I visited her, her family had arranged for her to move into an assisted living facility in the week ahead. She told me she was going to have a studio apartment and that her daughter had taken her back to her apartment from the nursing home earlier in the day to pick out the furniture she could take with her.

Among the pieces she was taking with her were her double bed, chest, a night table and her comfy chair, which had been moved into her room at the nursing home.

She said she had chosen two of the pictures on her walls to take with her. She noted one of her other daughters was an interior designer and she said that daughter would make the final decision as to whether they would stay or if other of her pictures would replace them.

As per the vintage Julia, she was very upbeat about the forthcoming change. She said she looked forward to the move and settling in to her new surroundings. Some curtains from her apartment at Palm Acres were going with her to make it look more like home.

Julia explained the assisted living place was divided up into neighborhoods with 13 residents living in each neighborhood. Each neighborhood had its own dining room and a sitting room. She said she wouldn't be going into the sitting room, however, because her sight is so poor she has to have her nose practically touching the TV to see it and needs a small TV like the one she'll have in her room in order to see the whole picture.

Julia had been lying down resting when I arrived to visit her and insisted on sitting up for our meeting, but I could tell she was getting tired sitting on the edge of the bed.

I told her I would leave so that she could lie down and rest again and bid adieu.

"You'll come visit me, won't you," she said brightly.

It was more of a statement than a question.

"Yes, I will," I assured her.

18

Chapter Eighteen

As We Grow Older

The most common infirmity among residents at Palm Acres would seem to be deafness. Many residents are hard of hearing and have hearing aids, but some don't always wear them. So one occasionally has to repeat what they say and/or raise their voice to be heard.

A few residents are afflicted with macular degeneration, a nasty condition that renders them unable to see well enough to make out who it is just a few feet from them.

There also is the occasional hip replacement or knee replacement.

A number of residents, and not just those recovering from surgery, use walkers to get around. But these are not like their grandmother's walker. They are pared down, light weight models, with hand brakes like racing bicycles and can be spun aground in a circle without moving forward. They also have a seat, making them usable as a chair, but can still be folded up to fit in the trunk of a car – a thoroughly modern walking aid.

It should be noted that not all residents using a walker do so because of a problem with their hips, knees legs or feet. Some people use them for balance – they can't maintain their balance without a walker to lean on.

There also are a lot of canes in use. Many of them are colorful designer numbers painted with flowers, stripes, circles, stars or any of a wide variety of decorations.

I soon became accustomed to seeing individuals with canes getting into their cars and driving away.

But I was more than a little taken aback when I saw a gentleman using a walker go over to his car, open the trunk, put the walker into the trunk, close it, then walk to the front door on the driver's side, open it and get into the car, then drive off.

A big enemy of everyone is the fall. And people fall all the time. More often than not, they suffer no more than bruises and sore muscles. But sometimes stitches are needed and occasionally they suffer more serious injuries, like broken bones, and wind up in the hospital or at the nursing home on the retirement community's campus.

The most feared infirmity, however, is dementia, whether Alzheimer's disease or something else. No one wants to lose any mental capacity.

Those with failing minds, or any debilitating illness, who are fortunate enough to have a spouse to look after them can continue to live in their home and do the usual everyday things for some time before needing to move into a nursing home.

Those without a spouse who are suffering from dementia or any debilitating illness can survive in their homes for a while with the help of aides several hours a day until their condition worsens to the point they need full-time care in a nursing home.

I never cease to be moved at seeing the loving care a wife or husband gives to their spouse who is physically or mentally handicapped. They often have been married for 50 years or more and look to be still as much in love as on their wedding day.

And a closing note…a great many old people are always cold, even in the heat of summer. When they enter a new building or a new room, they head for the thermostat with the intention of pushing it way up, much to the consternation of others present.

To thwart this activity in the clubhouse of Palm Acres, all thermostats in the hallways and public rooms of the building were put behind clear plastic enclosures under lock and key.

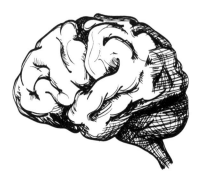

*"The most feared infirmity, however,
is dementia, whether Alzheimer's
disease or something else"*

19

Chapter Nineteen

The Health Care Center

Palm Acres has its own accredited health care center consisting of a clinic, a nursing home and a separate wing for dementia patients.

The clinic is staffed by a very capable nurse practitioner and serves not only residents of the retirement community but residents of the adjacent neighborhood.

The nursing home, likewise, accepts patients from the outside as well as residents of Palm Acres.

When a new member moves into Palm Acres, that person is entitled to 90 free days in the nursing home over their lifetime. For days spent in the nursing home beyond the first 90, they are charged one-half of the going daily rate charged by other nursing homes in the area. But that's only for members.

There are instances when one half of a couple is not a member.

People have to be in good health when they move into the retirement community to be accepted as a member. If one half of a couple is accepted as a member, but the spouse is so ill as to need nursing home care, Palm Acres will take the ailing spouse into the nursing home, if there is room, while the healthy spouse lives in an apartment, villa or house. The couple however will have to pay the standard rate for the housing of the healthy spouse plus the full cost for the nursing home care – no half rate. The health center doesn't offer assisted living but it has a program akin to that.

The lack of assisted living at the complex has long been regarded by a good many residents as a major hindrance keeping some prospective purchasers from actually buying a home in the Palm Acres development.

To meet that need, the health care professionals at the complex have devised a program that offers part-time in-home care which allows a resident to continue living independently in their apartment, villa or house for a longer time than otherwise.

Palm Acres had an assisted living facility at one time a long time ago, but it was closed down after nine months for lack of residents. Only two people lived there at the end and the retirement community was losing thousands of dollars on it every month.

It had been set up in one wing of the nursing home which has since been converted to office space for the health care professionals.

Over the years, the health professionals explored various other ways of providing assisted living.

They thought at one time of purchasing a three-bedroom cottage on the grounds and turning it into a group home for assisted living. But that idea was abandoned before it got very far.

Then they thought of converting the first floor of one of the development's larger apartment buildings, which has several living units complete with bathrooms and kitchens on that floor, into an assisted living facility. But that was abandoned because residents on the upper floors would have to walk through it to get home.

Finally, they came up with a reasonably close facsimile that wouldn't require a separate physical facility and would allow residents to continue enjoying independent living in their own apartment or cottage while also receiving the extra care they need.

The plan, now in place, calls for several residents to share home health aides – with four or five residents to one aide – who would assist them at those times of day when they need help.

For instance, one health aide may go to one resident's home in the morning to help him or her dress, fix their breakfast and help them with their medications, and then go to another resident and do the same, and so on until the aide's charges are all up and fed.

A home health aide would return to fix their lunches and similarly return in the evening to fix their dinners or help them with a dinner they ordered in from the main dining room if they were unable to go to the dining room to eat.

(The health center has its own kitchen and dining room to serve the patients there.)

Between meals a home health aide might come into the home to put laundry in the washer, come back later to put it in the dryer and come back yet again to fold it and put it away. And so on with other household and personal tasks.

Of course, a resident could hire a full-time health aide to look after only him or her for as many hours as are desired. But the cost of full-time help for one person is considerably more than if that person is willing to share the care of one aide with others.

The fledgling new program has been well received by its initial users by all accounts and is cautiously being called a success.

*"People have to be in good health
when they move into the retirement
community to be accepted as a member"*

20

Chapter Twenty
Moving In

I gave Julia about two weeks to get adjusted to her new home at the assisted living facility before visiting her, and when I did, she was in good spirits

Her one-room apartment was quite nice and had a private bath and built-in mini-kitchen with a sink and under-the-counter refrigerator.

Her bed was there along with a few other items that had been brought over from her old apartment in Palm Acres – including a side chair and a small wicker table next to it.

But her comfy chair had been left behind in the health center.

Being Julia, she had taken that matter into her own hands. She said she had called the plant manager at Palm Acres, who's one of the nicest guys on the planet, and asked him if he could help her get that chair – a lounger – over to her new place.

Without hesitation, he said, "Of course – when do you want it?" She said any time it was convenient for him to bring it over.

Julia said, much to her surprise, he was at the door of her apartment at 7 a.m. the next morning with the comfy chair in tow.

Her new home was now complete.

"he was at the door of her apartment at 7 a.m. the next morning with the comfy chair in tow"

21
Chapter Twenty-One
Open Meetings

Soon after moving into my retirement home, I began attending the meetings of the committees set up to recommend improvements and policy to management.

I was surprised to find that no other residents attended these meetings – with rare exceptions. In the northeastern state I moved from, no meeting of a condominium board or committee would go unattended by a great many of the residents. And my complex, for everything else it may be, basically is a condominium complex. I purchased my apartment, I own it, I pay property taxes on it, and I can sell it anytime I want.

All went smoothly at first, but then I encountered a problem with the chairman of one of the committees who didn't want me there and asked the administrator who was sitting in on the meeting if he had to let me stay. The administrator said he did. The administrator said any member of the community could attend any committee meeting.

"Alright," the chairman said, "we'll take a vote on it."

"No," the administrator said, "you won't. She stays."

That seemed to be that. But in time it turned into a bit of a dust-up which, in the end, clearly established the policy that any member can attend any committee meeting they wish – with the added proviso that the member, as a courtesy, notify the chairman in advance that they plan to attend.

All went well after that first standoff through much of the year with no complaints – to my knowledge – until budget time rolled around in the fall and a new executive director was in place. Then trouble bubbled up again in the same committee.

I was sitting in on a meeting of that committee, but when a member of the committee was going to make a presentation with his recommendation on what the committee should recommend to the committee preparing the budget for the next year for its share of that budget for the department it oversees, the chairman asked me to leave. I protested, but he was adamant. The new executive director was sitting in on this meeting too and I didn't feel this was the time or place to lodge a complaint. So I left.

I had been told I could not attend the meetings of the two committees formulating the budget while they were doing so, and could understand that and didn't protest.

I, however, continued to attend non-budget meetings of the committees and found unexpected support for my position in one of them. After two professionals made reports, the chairman asked each member for any comments they had on the reports or any other matter.

It should be noted that the executive director did not attend this meeting.

Midway around the U-shaped table, a woman member, who I had never seen before, said she was very upset that she had been denied admittance to the meeting of another committee. She said she had told others of her intention to go to the committee meeting, but before it took place she was told she could not attend the meeting.

She was dismayed, she said, adding it was her belief that any member should be allowed to attend any meeting.

Everyone else chimed in to say they thought It was terrible that she was blocked from attending the meeting and agreed every member should be allowed to attend any meeting.

Another member, who knew me, said they should ask me

about my experience since she knew I had been attending committee meetings. So they did. I told them that, with one exception, all the committees had been very welcoming. I did not identify the exception.

Another committee member asked the woman what committee had denied her attendance. When she replied, it was the same committee that had been trying to deny me attendance.

Still another member of the committee said that several years earlier he had wanted to attend the meetings of a different committee and had asked the then-long-time former executive director if he could do so. She told him, yes – that any member can go to any meeting they wish. His experience confirmed the long-standing open meetings policy.

At the next committee meeting I attended, the new executive director, a nifty lady who seemed to have settled comfortably into the job, chaired the meeting in the absence of the chairman and, at its conclusion, graciously asked me if I had any questions or comments as some of the other chairmen had been doing. I said thank you, but I had none. The next day she spoke at a meeting of the residents of my building in one of a series of "getting to know you" coffee gatherings, and she said what appeared to be the key to her acceptance of members attending committee meetings.

She said she had just come to realize we all owned our homes – whether apartment, villa or cottage. She said at the retirement communities where she previously worked, the residents did not own their homes.

Aha, I thought, she's got it.

The executive director subsequently told me she had consulted with one of the developers or the retirement community who's still involved with its management and he maintained it isn't exactly a condominium complex. Still, she assured me I could go to all the meetings, but asked that I – and anyone else who wants to do so – give the chairman a courtesy call to notify that person of the intent to attend their meeting.

Even so, it was not yet over. Faced with a confirmed open meetings policy, the chairman of the committee who objected to my presence, resigned as chairman rather than preside over a meeting with me or any other non-committee member sitting in.

22

Chapter Twenty-Two
Spirit of '45

Nothing in my memory nor in that of anyone I know has captivated the members of Palm Acres as the celebration of the 70th anniversary of the end of World War II. The event was celebrated with a display of residents' memorabilia from the war in the large display case in the clubhouse, with a parade of floats made from golf carts decorated by the various housing groups, a sumptuous luncheon of hamburgers, hot dogs and chicken grilled outdoors and served with all the picnic extras from corn on the cob to potato salad to watermelon, and finally, an evening concert with music of the era.

The day-long event, held a year in advance of the actual anniversary in 2015 as part of a national "Spirit of '45" " tour culminating the following August 14 (the date of the Japanese surrender), touched a soft spot in the entire retirement community's populous – those who served in the war and the younger residents who fought in later wars or no wars at all.

All the events of the day honored the men and women of Palm Acres and the deceased spouses of some who were veterans of World War II. There were generals, captains, lieutenants, ensigns, a fighter pilot and several nurses, among them.

Aging photographs, ranging from big to miniature, in the display case showed the veterans as young men and women heading off to war – including some who still look the same today.

They would fight through the Battle of the Bulge in Europe or on Tinian in the Solomon Islands in the Pacific theater – and in other similar places.

The exhibit contained the dog tag of the late husband of one of the residents and a Gen. Douglas MacArthur plate marking his role in fighting on "The Island Fortress of Corregidor." Another photo showed a newly married couple – a serviceman and his bride - walking out of a chapel under an arch of drawn swords held by other servicemen. There also was a photo of a nurse who was a physical therapist sitting with a group of young men – all amputees – whom she had helped in their recovery.

There was a folded American flag that had flown over the nation's capitol and had been presented to the parents of a serviceman who had died in the Battle of the Bulge.

A screaming banner headline in the Dec. 11, 1941, Nashville Banner announced "Congress Declares War Against Germany and Italy." Another screaming headline in the Aug. 15, 1945, issue of the Philadelphia Inquirer declared simply "PEACE" followed by a smaller second deck saying, "Truman announces Jap Surrender, Ends Fighting."

The cover of a Time magazine carried the picture of Robert Murphy, the first postwar ambassador to Japan and the great uncle of a resident.

Who knew that after all these years there would be so many momentos.

A pair of veterans were taking in the exhibit when one said to the other, "My mother saved every letter that I wrote home." The sight prompted many such comments.

A special booklet prepared by the retirement community's management reported the responses received to a query they had put out asking where were you when you heard the war had ended. It made for interesting and memorable reading.

The housing groups – each apartment and villa building and the two cottage developments – went all out in decorating their floats and had a lot of fun doing it.

The floats were accompanied in the parade by several open cars – including a vintage World War II era Jeep – carrying World War II veterans along the route, and by a marching unit with a mix of veterans, spouses of veterans and workers in the complex related to veterans.

The day concluded with a wonderful concert presented by the Big Band from the neighborhood next door – all volunteers but extremely professional.

In remembrance of the veterans being honored, the band devoted its two-hour performance to tunes of the 30s and 40s. We tapped our feet and sometimes hummed along with such numbers as "In the Mood," "String of Pearls," "Swinging Shepherd Blues," "Satin Doll," and "Moonlight Serenade."

As we were all commenting during a break in the music on what a great day it had been, a woman sitting at my table remarked, "I think it has brought us all closer together as a family."

Indeed, it had.

*"Nothing in my memory has captivated
the members of Palm Acres as the
celebration of the 70th anniversary of
the end of World War II"*

23

Chapter Twenty-Three
What To Look For

One of the biggest mistakes folks who plan on moving to a retirement community make is to wait too long to do it. If in the meantime "something happens," that could limit their choice in places to live as many upscale retirement communities expect their move-ins to be healthy able-bodied seniors.

If one's health declines after moving into a retirement community, arrangements usually can be made to accommodate their disability.

Having said that, I confess to waiting five years before moving into the retirement community that I chose. I fell in love with my retirement community the first time I saw it. But there were two problems.

The first problem was that it was the first retirement community that I had visited and I had yet to do my due diligence by visiting other retirement communities as well.

I addressed this issue by visiting a different retirement community during my travels each year when I took my vacation so I had a basis for comparison.

The second problem was that I wasn't "ready." I wasn't ready to give up my home, my work, my friends, my town – my happy life where I was living. But after a couple of very harsh and difficult winters where I had trouble getting around, I became "ready."

I actually knew in my heart several years earlier that one day I would move into a retirement community, which is what brought me that first day to the place where I now live. So I would advise anyone with the slightest notion that they might one day want to move into a retirement community to begin checking them out on their annual vacation.

Things to look for in your search for just the right place:

--If the retirement community lies in a hurricane-prone area, does it have an evacuation plan, not only for you but for your pet if you have one, with buses to take you to a safe inland location if your town is threatened by an approaching hurricane.

--Is the retirement community solvent. Check the financials if available. How much debt is it carrying, if any. When is the debt, if there is any, scheduled to be retired.

-- Is there an annual assessment. If so how much is it.

--What type of ownership does the retirement community offer. Is it like a condominium where you buy and can sell your unit at any time or is it the type where you buy in over a period of time, such as four years, and where you can get some money back if you leave after one, two or three years, but are locked in after four years with no refund if you choose to leave. There also are some rental properties coming on the market.

--Does the retirement community have its own nursing home. Does it have a clinic to deal with lesser ailments and medical needs. Does it offer assisted living.

--If the retirement community offers "continuing care," ask what exactly that means. It may mean truly lifetime care at no cost to you, but it also may mean only a few months of care at no cost but with a reduced charge from the normal rate for additional time.

--What form of management does the retirement community have. Who owns it. Where does control over it lie. Is an outside management company employed to run it.

--If you are ready to buy a unit or buy into the retirement community, ask to see a disclosure statement before signing any papers. There could be issues – as major as stucco pulling away from the walls or as minor as smoke remediation having been necessary to deal with the aftermath of a former occupant who was a heavy smoker.

--Don't hesitate to make an offer below the asking price for the unit you want. In many instances, it's negotiable.

--If you are going to own the unit, ask what the property taxes on it are.

--Ask if tipping is allowed, even expected. That can significantly increase your monthly cost. Tipping is prohibited in my retirement community, but at Christmas time residents are expected to make a meaningful contribution to a holiday fund for employees.

--What kind of transportation does the retirement community provide. Is it by private car at any time of day that you choose or is it scheduled bus trips to various destinations. Does the retirement community charge extra for such transportation.

--Does the retirement community charge extra for delivering "to go" dinner meals to the door of your unit. That can add up if you use home delivery often.

--Are meals served sit-down style in the dining room or is service for some meals cafeteria-style.   .

--If you want to attend meetings of member committees – those committees made up of residents of the retirement community – are you permitted to do so.

--Is there adequate parking space.

--Is there flooding on the grounds.

--And finally, what kind of activities are offered. Are they going to be enough to keep you as busy as you want to be and happy.

About the Author

 Sherry Conohan, now a free-lance writer, is an award winning journalist who brings five decades of experience as a newspaper and wire service reporter, editorial writer and columnist to every assignment she undertakes.

A graduate of the University of Missouri School of Journalism, she worked for the United Press International wire service in four bureaus – Jefferson City, Mo.; Des Moines, Iowa; Chicago and New York - and several newspapers over the years.

Sherry is now retired from the Asbury Park Press in New Jersey, but keeps active as a free-lancer. She writes regularly for a monthly magazine and contributes occasional articles to a daily newspaper. This is her first book.

33567532R00040

Made in the USA
Charleston, SC
18 September 2014